NATURE
AND EXISTENCE

Other Books by Walt McLaughlin:

Forest Under My Fingernails
Reflections and Encounters on Vermont's Long Trail
(narrative)

Arguing With the Wind
A Spiritual Journey into the Alaskan Wilderness
(narrative)

Backcountry Excursions
Venturing into the Wild Regions of the Northeast
(short narratives)

Worldly Matters
(essays and short narratives)

A Hungry Happiness
(poetry)

Edited by Walt McLaughlin:

A Natural Wisdom
Gleanings from the Journals of Henry David Thoreau
(selected prose)

The Laws of Nature
Excerpts from the Writings of Ralph Waldo Emerson
(selected prose)

NATURE
AND EXISTENCE

by

Walt McLaughlin

Wood Thrush Books

Printed by: Van Volumes
                A Division of TigerPress
                155 Industrial Drive
                Northampton, Massachusetts 01060

Published by: Wood Thrush Books
                85 Aldis Street
                St. Albans, Vermont 05478

ISBN 978-0-9798720-4-4

Table of Contents

NATURE
AND EXISTENCE

The Known and the Unknown

The first philosopher was a shaman gazing deep into the prehistoric sky, trying to extract truth from the sun, moon and stars. By then our kind had already developed a sense of time – an acute awareness of birth, death, and the succession of events between. By then we had been burying our dead, painting pictures on cave walls, and engaging in other ritualistic behavior for many, many generations. The shaman observed the world about him, gave it some thought, then made his proclamations. He told his fellow primitives that, above all else, the world is a magical, mysterious place. Fifteen thousand years ago, as the great sheets of ice were retreating north and the landscape was changing dramatically, no one had any doubts about this. The shaman was only stating the obvious.

The celestial bodies passing overhead marked time. Somehow they controlled day and night, the seasons, and other natural cycles. As humankind gradually developed agricultural societies, understanding these cycles became increasingly more important. It was up to the shaman, now a high priest, to make sense of these things. So the high priest carefully studied the sky overhead, creating calendars and charts. The high priest became the arbiter of all the knowledge locked in the heavens. And religion was born.

"Religion is the attempt to fill the gap between the known and the unknown," an obscure philosopher named Rudolf

Jordan wrote back in the 1950s. This is no less true today than it was thousands of years ago, when the first civilizations arose. In that regard, we are all religious to some extent, cultivating elaborate worldviews by which we live our lives. Some of these worldviews are utterly fantastic; others are quite rational. All of them grapple with the unknown. Since we aren't privy to absolute knowledge, we do what we can to fill in the blanks. We assess the world around us then take a leap of faith. We must believe in *something*, whether it's a priest's proclamation, a sacred text, or an apparently logical argument. Belief itself, regardless what it's based upon, is universal. No cognizant creature can function without it.

Reason is a powerful tool. There can be no science without reason, and science is precisely what has propelled our kind from the African savanna to deep space. Science is the microchip. It is also the stone chipped into a cutting instrument many thousands of years ago. Science is the campfire created from scratch, the steam engine, the blast furnace, and the nuclear reactor. The explosion of scientific and technological innovation during the past few hundred years clearly illustrates what the rational mind can do. Consequently, there are those who trust reason and reason alone. But even belief in reason is still a belief, and all beliefs require a leap of faith.

When Nicolas Copernicus first considered the possibility that the Earth moves around the Sun, even he thought it was an absurd idea. But he made his calculations and convinced himself that this was indeed the case. To avoid the storm of controversy that this radically new idea would generate, he waited until he was on his deathbed before publishing his findings. Common sense is hard to buck. At that time, people naturally assumed that the Earth was the center of the universe, with the sun, moon and stars moving around it in perfect harmony.

Fourteen hundred years earlier, a Greco-Egyptian mathematician named Ptolemy had taken pains to explain the intricate movements of celestial bodies across the night sky, thus proving that the Earth was stationary. By the time Copernicus and those like him were considering other possibilities, the Church and its scholars had fully embraced the Ptolemaic worldview and had inexorably linked it to the Holy Scriptures. Therefore the sun-centered idea had to be stopped. It was heretical. In 1600 a loudmouthed, renegade scholar named Giordano Bruno went around advocating the Copernican heresy, so the Church burned him at the stake for it. But facts are difficult to suppress. The observations that Galileo Galilei made of Jupiter and its moons, through a new invention called the telescope, lent greater credence to the sun-centered idea. In 1632 Galileo abandoned Latin, the language of scholars, and published his findings in Italian, the language of regular folks, thus sending the controversy into the streets.

"May God forgive Galileo," Pope Urban VIII said, as the aging Italian astronomer went before the Inquisition for popularizing the Copernican heresy. And that's when Galileo realized he was in trouble. He thought the pope – an intelligent man who had discussed the matter at length with him in private – would back him up. But the pope thought it best to "go along with common opinion" whether it was true or not. Under the thinly veiled threat of torture, the Inquisition eked an admission from Galileo that his findings were wrong. Then he was allowed to live out the rest of his days in relative peace. All the same, the facts remained the facts. It was just a matter of time before this radically new idea of sun-centeredness supplanted the old way of seeing things.

By the end of the 17th Century, once the English mathematician Isaac Newton had published his seminal work on gravitation, most scientists and scholars had embraced the Copernican worldview. Today it's a given. Today we all know that the Earth revolves around the Sun, right? Wrong. The Flat Earth Society, boasting 3,000 members, still thinks the sun-centered idea is a great lie fabricated by evildoers to discredit the Holy Scriptures. For some people, it seems, there are never enough facts to dislodge cherished beliefs.

What does all this tell us? Only that the most widely-held worldviews can change, given sufficient time and information. Granted, there will always be a few holdouts, but when enough people finally accept what's going on, humanity as a whole adapts to a whole new way of seeing things. After all, adaptation is what our species does best.

Intellectual revolutions take time. "The most valued facts arrive unexpectedly," the naturalist Chet Raymo said, "And nakedly unadorned." When these facts first arrive, only a few people take notice. Then a few more people notice, then a few more, and on and on like that until the facts become irresistible. In this way, collective human understanding advances. In this way, the known pushes back the unknown.

"I think therefore I am," Rene Descartes said, thus giving birth to an utterly rationalistic worldview. Other thinkers came along shortly thereafter with similar philosophies – some upholding Cartesian notions of pure abstraction; others arguing more in favor of knowledge rooted in sensory experience. Then Immanuel Kant conjured up "synthetic a priori" – knowledge synthesized from both abstraction and sense experience – a concept interpreted loosely as intuition. And the argument shifted to higher ground.

Whether or not such a thing as intuition actually exists remains a subject of intense debate. Few concepts are more misrepresented or maligned. Some people consider intuition an emotional alternative to thinking. Others treat it as a supernatural phenomenon. Still others dismiss it as mere short-circuit in the reasoning process. But Kant's intention was clear when he first coined his term "synthetic a priori." He thought it possible to know that something is true *before* it is rendered a scientific fact. When you think about it, this kind of knowledge is the basis of all belief, of all philosophy and religion. Every worldview has at its core a set of carefully guarded assumptions. Where do these assumptions come from? Regardless of their source, assumptions always require a leap of faith. Ah, back to that again.

To many people, especially those of us who like to wander through wild country on a regular basis, the world is just as magical and mysterious today as it was when our stone-chipping ancestors lived. In some ways it is even more mysterious, since our current knowledge of both the subatomic realm and the universe at large has grown in ways that no shaman could ever have imagined. Mother Nature has never been as awe-inspiring as she is today, and the more we learn about her, the more we realize how much more there is to learn. Our grasp of the real is still in its early stages, or so it seems to those of us who wander and wonder. Humankind is just beginning to understand the world. All the same, there are those among us who believe we will soon be able to dismiss the unknown once and for all.

"I do not agree with the view that the universe is a mystery," the renowned astrophysicist Stephen Hawking once wrote, "Something that one can have intuition about but never fully analyze or comprehend." Many other intelligent, rational men and women share this view. To them the word "intuition" has little or no meaning, and religion is but a crutch for the feeble-minded. They believe reason alone is the hope of the world, and that the unknown is just a dark tunnel from which we will ultimately emerge triumphant. But I find this belief hard to swallow. I cannot imagine there ever coming a day when we will know everything there is to know, when a revolution in thinking of the same magnitude as the Copernican Revolution will no longer be possible.

Our lives are enhanced by mystery, not diminished by it. We are no less human for standing awestruck before nature. In fact, we are human *because* we wonder, *because* we look around us and ask the questions for which there are no definitive answers. Are we Mother Nature's children or something else altogether? Does order or chaos reign in the universe? Does God exist or is the physical world all there is? These and other fundamental questions weigh heavily upon us. Some people embrace preexisting worldviews so that they can readily dismiss these questions and get on with their lives. Others ponder such matters to the point of absurdity. It's all a matter of choice, I suppose. But we are all philosophers to some extent – thinking, self-aware creatures set loose in the world.

Both the known and the unknown have been with us since the dawn of time. One could argue that an awareness of what we know and don't know is precisely what makes us human. Whether it is or not, it is safe to say that the unknown will remain with us a while longer.

The Quest for Meaning

Knowledge is power. This is a truism in the Age of Information, when the free flow of images and ideas is radically changing the world around us. This is why most of us place such a high premium on education – why there are so many books, websites, seminars and classrooms. But knowledge for its own sake isn't universally valued. The Chinese philosopher Chuang Tzu once said: "The sage hatches no schemes, so what use has he for knowledge?" That ancient lotus-eater made a good point. What good is knowledge if one doesn't make use of it? Why should one bother learning anything if one isn't interested in getting ahead in the world? And what is it exactly that we are trying to achieve? These are questions revealing the assumptions we all make about the world and our place in it. These are dangerous questions to ask, no doubt.

Growing up in Catholic schools, I was forced to memorize then recite the church's catechism. In the public school system, I was given a similar form of indoctrination regarding civic matters – the pledge of allegiance and all that. These exercises were designed to instill in me a proper sense of values. They didn't take, though. Instead the bits of information I was force-fed by educators only whetted my appetite for knowing, really knowing what life is all about. But the deeply probing questions that arose from my growing appetite were too often met by teacher's frowns. That's when I knew I'd crossed some kind of invisible line. That's when it dawned on me that I'd have to look elsewhere for the answers to life's most pertinent questions.

I was a strange kid, no doubt, driven by forces that didn't seem to trouble anyone else. In my mid-teens, I slipped out of school on a regular basis and went to the public library. No truant officer ever thought to look for me there. I was hungry for the kind of knowledge that traditional education couldn't supply. I wanted to know why things are the way they are. I had questions, all kinds of questions, about the world and the way it is organized – questions that no one around me would answer. I read Chinese philosophy, the Holy Scriptures and their various interpretations, other religious texts, books about great thinkers and teachers, and plenty of esoteric nonsense. The path to wisdom, I soon learned, is a long and winding one with plenty of dead ends along the way. I read anything that offered the slightest hint whatsoever regarding God's intentions, the destiny of humankind, and the grand design of the cosmos. And for the most part, I was disappointed. I remained hungry – starving, in fact – for some clue as to what it is all about.

When finally I ended up alone in a church in the middle of the night, down on my knees and howling "Why?" from a place deep inside me, I knew I had *really* crossed the line. In that moment I became Adam biting the apple, Moses running off to the desert. And there was no going back. I left that church building feeling hungrier than I'd ever felt before, and less certain about God, the world, and myself than I'd ever thought possible. That's when it occurred to me that I was on the path to spiritual oblivion. Either that or I was going mad.

The psychiatrist who treated me in the months that followed saw a silver lining in my spiritual/psychological crisis. He said I was lucky to be addressing these matters at such an early age, before I was well into a life that I didn't really want. He made it clear that my hunger was not all that unusual, that many people find themselves searching for something to believe in – something cutting deep, going beyond established credos. I told him he was full of it. Yeah, I was a feisty little egghead back then. So more out of frustration than helpfulness, he suggested that I read Jean Paul Sartre's *Being and Nothingness*. I skimmed through a copy of that weighty tome then dismissed both Sartre's endless ramblings and my shrink's advice as so much meaningless blather. I wanted answers. They only posed more questions.

College wasn't much better as far as getting answers went. At first I was foolish enough to think that that old Greek philosopher, Aristotle, had it all figured out. It certainly seemed that way when I first read his work. But the more I read, the more I realized that neither Aristotle nor his rival Plato, nor any other great thinker since them had cornered *the truth*. When I expressed this sentiment in a classroom one day, during a course on the history of Western philosophy, the professor responded very calmly between puffs on this pipe: "But you're too young to be cynical," and everyone in the room laughed. Everyone, that is, except me.

A short while later, I found a like-minded other in a slender volume called *The Myth of Sisyphus*. It's author, Albert Camus, knew all too well the terrible hunger of unknowing. "One day the 'why' arises," he wrote, "and everything begins in that weariness tinged with amazement." Yeah, he knew. That is why I became so fascinated with his work during the last days of my formal education. "Reason and the irrational lead to the same preaching," Camus also said. That much I'd already learned the hard way. So now, I figured, it was time to go

15

beyond the preaching and look for something more tangible.

My declaration of spiritual and intellectual independence occurred a year and a half before reading Camus, actually, when I tossed my combat boots down the dormitory hallway in a fit of rage. I was finishing up a semester at the time. I had been polishing my combat boots when suddenly it dawned on me that I had no business serving a country whose values were not my own. So I quit pretending to be an ROTC cadet, a Catholic, or a member of any other group. I grew a beard, grabbed a beat-up old Boy Scout pack then hitchhiked from Ohio to British Columbia looking for something to sink my teeth into. I found hope on the shoulder of Mt. Baker in the North Cascades, surrounded by wildness, near the border between Canada and Washington State. There I caught a glimpse of something that doesn't exist in books – something so real that I could find no words for it. But I caught a glimpse and didn't forget. And that kept me going until I left the college campus with a degree in Nothingness firmly in hand.

In his book, *Man's Search for Meaning*, Victor Frankl makes it clear that the search for meaning as "a primary force" in one's life and not just a rationalization for instinctual drives. In this regard, most psychologists, philosophers, and theologians have gotten it wrong. While Frankl was interned in a Nazi concentration camp, he gave meaning and existence serious consideration. I could relate to that, having pondered these matters long enough myself to question everything, even the value of living. But it doesn't take a concentration camp or the contemplation of suicide to realize that meaning is the driving force behind everything we do. All you need is a touch of spiritual/intellectual honesty – a moment in time when you stop listening to all the bullshit, especially your own, and take a long, hard look at the world.

The hunger begins when suddenly you think that maybe, just maybe, there is more to existence than meets the eye, when you consider the possibility that life isn't just an elaborate game to be lost or won. What should you do then? Meaning isn't something you get from a book or a classroom. It can't be won in a contest, nor can anyone can give it to you. Meaning isn't on the front page of the morning newspaper, can't be worn around the neck like a medallion, and it certainly won't come like an obedient dog when you call it. Meaning can't be placed on a shelf like a trophy, or be squirreled away in a safe deposit box like a bar of gold. If gurus answer us in riddles when we ask them: "What is the meaning of life?" that's only because they know that meaning isn't transferable. What works for one person won't necessarily work for the next.

I suspect that most people focus on happiness instead of meaning because happiness seems easier to obtain. We all know what it feels like to be happy. As children, we pursued this feeling with a vengeance. As adults, most people still do. But happiness is fleeting and tied circumstances more beyond our control than any of us are willing to admit. Walk the streets on the first warm, sunny day right after a long, hard winter and see how many people are smiling. Note the change in yourself and those around you since yesterday's cold rain. It's good to be happy – no one will deny that. But how well does the pursuit of happiness get you through hard times? That's when you need something more substantial.

The quest for meaning is what every worthwhile philosophy is about. It is the essence of all true spirituality, as well, even though the catechisms of organized religions often lead elsewhere. The quest for meaning is a long and arduous journey – one that seems utterly futile at times.

And for this reason, it isn't something I would recommend, especially to those looking to get ahead in the world. But this is beside the point, really. The quest for meaning begins in precisely that moment when a pilgrim rejects advice and strikes out on his or her own. It begins when a truly hungry heart abandons everything but the hunger itself. Then nature takes its course. Then the pilgrim is in God's hands and the world is a wide-open road.

Wild, Wilderness, Bewilderment

The moment I set eyes upon Linton Lake, I knew there was something special about the place. Any thoughts I may have had to the contrary were quickly dispelled by the bald eagle screaming from its perch high above the water. While looking at a map of the area, it slowly dawned on me that beyond the lake stretched a country wilder than any I'd ever seen before. That's when I felt an overwhelming urge to keep going. I wanted to dive deep into that sprawling wilderness and experience things I'd only read about in books. But it wasn't going to happen that day. I had a girlfriend waiting patiently for me at the trailhead two miles back. Besides, I wasn't the least bit prepared for an extended backcountry excursion. So I turned away, promising myself that I would venture out there as soon as possible.

Several years earlier, I had flown to Seattle, Washington and taken up residence there with every intention of exploring the nearby Cascade Mountains. I did just that during the months that followed, but never for more than a day at a time. Then I moved back east, preoccupied with more mundane matters. In the spring of 1980, I returned to the Pacific Northwest with my girlfriend. We landed in Eugene, Oregon. That's when I first saw Linton Lake – a pristine body of water situated along the northernmost edge of the Three Sisters Wilderness. Two months later, I stuffed an old Boy Scout rucksack full of supplies and went into that wilderness for a week. It was my first big solo trek into the wild. And that's when I became truly bewildered.

At six thousand feet, there was still snow on the ground despite the long summer sun. I wasn't accustomed to hiking in conditions like these, so I followed another hiker's tracks cutting through the snow. I soon lost the trail. While keeping panic at bay, I climbed a small mountain and triangulated my position with map and compass. That put me back on the trail again, but not for long. The next day, a thrush sang from a low-hanging branch while I was taking a lunch break. Suddenly I felt the same urge I'd felt at Linton Lake months earlier – the urge to go deeper. So I abandoned the beaten path. I dropped down into the nearby Linton Meadows. Then I wandered through country too wild and beautiful to be anything but a dream. I didn't awaken, though. Instead I just kept wandering, from one meadow to another, wandering aimlessly in some kind of daze until finally I made camp next to a small stream. And there I stayed for two days. I stayed put long enough for the wild to overwhelm me. I stayed long enough to feel the presence of the divine in the surrounding landscape.

What happens in one's head at such times? Three decades later, I am still mystified by the mist that curled around the mountains rising above those meadows. I am still amazed by the tremendous racket the animals made as they gathered in the meadows around midnight, and how clearly visible they were beneath the moon. I let chipmunks overrun my camp. A bear came around, sniffed at the food bag I'd slung in nearby trees, but caused me no trouble. At one point during the outing, I saw a mountain lion licking its lips, uneasy about my presence on its turf. But the lion left me alone, as well. Even now, many years later, I can still see the spark of wildness burning in its green eyes. Even now, I am still astonished by that magnificent country. I remain mystified by its unspeakable beauty, utterly bewildered by it. That six-day immersion changed me. My angst-ridden search for meaning ended abruptly in mountain meadows. After that, my hunger to understand the world was just a matter of trying to grasp on some rational level what I had just learned viscerally from the wild.

Would I call what happened to me at Linton Meadows a mystical experience? I cringe whenever I hear that word. It all depends upon how you define "mystical," I suppose. To most people the word suggests something going beyond the normal scope of things. It suggests supernatural forces at work. But I don't think that's the right way to explain such encounters.

In his book, *Mysticism & Philosophy*, W. T. Stace talks at length about the naturalistic principle. According to this principle, nothing occurs outside of nature no matter how bizarre it might seem. All things are natural. But even a simple statement like this is presumptuous. We can't know everything there is to know about the world, so who's to say what is natural and what is not? It seems the word "mystical" is fraught with assumptions about the nature of reality, about nature itself. We're on shaky ground here, to be sure.

Yes, I was completely overwhelmed by wildness when I ventured alone into that coniferous rainforest blanketing Oregon's Cascade Mountains. Yes, I was bewildered in the truest sense of the word. Even now, after all these years, I still can't fully explain what happened to me there. The best I can do is this: the wild revealed itself to me in the Linton Meadows in a way that I couldn't ignore. And I reveled in it. The wild emerged from a place deep within me during my brief sojourn there and, as a consequence, those meadows became something sacred to me. A part of me went wild during that trip and has stayed that way ever since. Mystical experience? There is probably a better way to describe encounters like this. Unfortunately, I haven't found it yet. Words fail to convey what happens at such times.

Martin Buber was no stranger to mystical experience. "How can I withstand the infinity of this moment?" he once asked. "You can't," I would have said to that old Hasidic philosopher if I had met him. We are completely overwhelmed in that moment and regardless what we say or think afterward, the mystical exists only in the present, in the *here and now*. It has no place in the regular sequence of events. Later on, we try to sort things out. Firmly rooted in time and space again, we try to make sense of those fleeting encounters. But the mystical exists only in absolute immediacy, where our true natures take flight. The Eternal Other rises before us like a great void, and into that Otherness all sense of self disappears. It is utterly bewildering. Or perhaps I should say, it becomes bewildering in retrospect, when we return to the mundane realm of day-to-day living, wondering what just happened.

Welcome to the wild. It disrupts the perfect lawn with a dandelion. It surprises you with a downpour right after all the weather forecasters promised you a sunny day. The wild ocean tosses your mighty ship like a cork in a bathtub. The wild earth trembles and down goes your skyscraper. If the wild night sky doesn't make your jaw drop, that's only because you aren't paying attention. The wild is everywhere, farther out into space than you can imagine and deep, deep within you. Only in fleeting moments, in unexpected flashes of insight, do we become aware of it. The rest of our lives, we simply muddle along, oblivious to the incredible world all around us.

Like John Muir, I used to pine for a simpler time when the first people roamed the earth, when the planet was largely untouched and everything was fraught with possibility. But extended trips into wild country change that. After taking enough backcountry excursions, Muir said, "I have discovered that I also live in creation's dawn." In other words, the world begins anew every time we find ourselves immersed in the wild. Muir was quick to learn this. Now I too see things this way.

Despite all the tragedy reported in the news, the world is more beautiful to me now than it ever was. Every day the wild surprises me. What I first saw from the shoulder of Mt. Baker as a young vagabond, and what overwhelmed me at Linton Meadows a few years later, now exists all around me. I see it in parks, in the roadside ditches, along inconspicuous waterways, and all around town. I see it in my own back yard. It exists in the ground beneath my feet, in the air I breathe and the sky overhead. It is virtually everywhere.

We live in a truly remarkable world – as remarkable as it is beautiful. Since this planet is all we know, it is easy to take for granted. But the miracle of it can still be grasped now and then, in brief moments of insight. All we have to do is get out of the day-to-day routine long enough to see it. All we have to do is open our eyes.

The Sharp Edge of What-Is

There is more to the world than meets the eye. Perception is reality, some people will tell you, but they're only trying to sell you something – a fixed worldview, a bill of goods, or a well-crafted lie. Truth is, nothing is more difficult to grasp than the reality of the world. Reality eludes us as we go about our day-to-day affairs. We rise from our beds in the morning to eat, work, play, laugh, cry and interact with others, but generally muddle through our waking hours as if sleepwalking. We live mostly in our dreams and only on rare occasion catch a glimpse of What-Is.

How can we know reality apart from our ideas about it? This is something philosophers have been pondering for thousands of years. "You cannot understand unless you have experienced," a Sufi mystic named Simab once said, thus giving full weight to the power direct encounter. But experience is only meaningful when we are open to the lessons it teaches. A person can sail around the world for years and be no wiser than he or she was when stepping off the wharf. There are those who crowd their lives with experiences yet remain on their deathbeds as clueless about What-Is as those who never tried anything new. A mind open to possibilities is critical to understanding.

Shortly after I moved to Vermont, I went into the Green Mountains and found plenty of wildness there. The New

24

England landscape is not as grand as the Oregon Cascades, the Canadian Rockies, or other places I have visited out west, but it harbors the wild nonetheless. On every day hike, overnighter and extended excursion into the woods, I came to know it. I sought out the wild and cultivated it in me until the line between self and other began to blur. I found sacred places in Vermont woods, miles from any road, and slowly came to appreciate their power. I took up backcountry fishing, learning the ways of wild trout, biting insects and dense brush, slowly surrendering to the grand design. But always I held back, keeping something in reserve: a part of myself jealously and unconsciously guarded.

It is easy to experience What-Is when you are deep in a wilderness area, away from the distractions of the mundane. To make sense of those experiences afterward, well, that is another matter. The problem with any excursion into deep woods is that it's temporary and therefore forgettable. Later on, What-Is fades in the mounting details of day-to-day life. Making it stick requires an exceptional undertaking, I concluded after much deliberation. What I needed was an outing that would leave a permanent mark – one that would *really* rattle my cage.

In the summer of 1992, I had a bush pilot drop me in a remote corner of Southeast Alaska. I had come to appreciate wildness in all its forms and wanted to spend a little time in a place where it was the rule not the exception. In that regard the Endicott River Wilderness did not disappoint. I spent two weeks alone there, completely out of contact with humanity except for the occasional bush plane flying overhead. I spent most of my time interacting with ravens, eagles, bears, and other wild animals, learning things about the world that I'd somehow missed during my

25

first thirty-six years on this planet. I learned a few things about myself, as well. In fact, I went in search of wild reality and got more, much more than I bargained for.

The wild is alive and well in Vermont's Green Mountains, but exists there only in pockets. Even when I lived in Oregon, I had to leave an elaborate network of roads and hike *into* the wilderness. But in Alaska, you go *out* to it. This is obvious to anyone flying over that great expanse. Still I think it's possible to visit Alaska, nibble at its edges, and not be profoundly affected by it. Being alone deep in the bush is another matter, though. In the sprawling Alaskan bush, you can easily forget about the civilized world. In the bush, there is only you and the wild stretching in every direction as far as you can see.

I went into the bush with a burning desire to witness raw existence – reality apart from any philosophical interpretation of it. I went there hoping for more than a mere glimpse of What-Is. I wanted a great big dollop of it and that's exactly what I got. But I didn't like it at first. I recoiled from the bush as if I'd been stung. I recoiled because it didn't fit into the nice, tidy worldview I had been cultivating since I was a teen. Fact is, the Alaskan bush wasn't much like anything I'd read in books, and absolutely nothing like what others had told me. I resisted it for the same reason that human beings have been plowing fields, herding animals, and building towns for millennia. Civilization is the buffer we create between oblivion and ourselves. When I stood face-to-face with brute survival, I didn't like it at all. A hard truth was shoved in my face: the wild is as indifferent about me as it is about all life forms. Individuals, whether they are flowering plants, insects, salmon, grouse or people, are expendable. Nature persists, certainly, but its particulars do not matter. And while I was in the bush, I was just another one of those particulars.

Long before spending time in the Alaskan bush, I knew on some level that the wild has a sharp edge to it. But it didn't register deep in my gut until I stumbled upon the remains of a moose scattered across a gravel riverbank. As I squatted in the middle of those remains, it suddenly occurred to me that I could meet the same fate tomorrow. I might stumble into a thousand-pound brown bear, upset him somehow, and then lose the contest that would ensue. The wolves would tear my carcass apart when they found it, until I looked just like this. The ravens would pick my bones clean without giving the matter a second thought. No crime would be committed. No one would be hunted down by the authorities and put in jail as a consequence. Life would go on. My flesh would nourish other creatures for a while, so the wild would be served. All the same, this wasn't the wild that I was looking for. This certainly wasn't what I had in mind when I stood on the shoulder of Mt. Baker a decade and a half earlier, catching that first glimpse of something divine.

"Listen to the voice of the wind," the poet Rilke once wrote, "And the ceaseless message that forms itself out of silence." I have been in the bush and have listened to the wind howling through the Endicott River Valley for days on end. I have heard it speak and have argued with it, seething with anger about the world I have found. No, I didn't like the way the world was organized and I made it a point to tell God as much while feeding sticks to a campfire one night. I criticized His handiwork while fueling my fire. I was ready to cry, "Foul!" the moment some toothy creature emerged from the darkness. Yet I was confused, a few hours later, when the sun rose high in the sky, to find myself still standing there unmolested over a pile a cooling embers. I was exhausted, bewildered once again, mystified by nature's endless mysteries. I was exhausted, yes, but no

27

longer angry. Then I went to bed fully aware that I had just lost the argument. What-Is did not care whether I approved or not, and it was not going to bend itself to my will. I could either accept things are they are or entertain whatever delusions I so desired. Those were my choices.

This wild world is both harsh and beautiful. To a moralist like me, this reality is difficult to accept. I want the world to be a better place for all parties involved. I want the bear and the bald eagle to prosper, along with the deer, the songbird and every other creature. I want all living things, amoeba to man, to achieve some sustainable level of mutually supportive existence. I want life on this planet of ours to achieve perfect balance and stay that way indefinitely. But the wild doesn't share this sentiment. Nature doesn't care which particulars come and go. It doesn't even care if this beautiful planet of ours becomes a lifeless rock then falls into the sun. After all, there are other planets. The wild will persist and that's all that matters.

The German philosopher Friedrich Nietzsche came to a conclusion similar to mine back in the 19th Century, but used it as an excuse to dismiss morality altogether – as if wild nature's indifference ought rightly to be matched by our own. In a world where every individual is expendable, Nietzsche told us, the only thing that matters is individual power. So the will to power became his religion, his morality. If wild nature is heartless and we are a part of nature, then we too should be heartless, or so Nietzsche reasoned. But I'm not convinced that anything about humanity can be inferred from the struggle for existence that is so pervasive in the wild. After all, we are acutely aware creatures, and that awareness is precisely what sets us apart from the rest of existence. It's not just a matter of being smarter than your average ape. From our acute awareness comes all sense of right and wrong. Morality arises not from wild nature, but from human nature. So the big questions are these: What are we to make of ourselves? What are we to make of the world?

That great lover of nature, Henry David Thoreau, once wrote: "Heaven is under our feet as well as over our heads." This is true, no doubt, but Hell also exists here. Fact is, everything that we call Heaven and Hell is as much a part of this world as we are. It's largely a matter of circumstances, which change as quickly as the weather. Still I am madly in love with this world, as much if not more than Henry was. I emerged from the bush shaken to the core by the wild, yet no less amazed by the forces of nature at work on this watery planet of ours. I wouldn't want to live anywhere else.

No doubt there are those who wouldn't mind living completely indoors, whether it's here, on some other planet, or on a vessel deep in space. But I for one revel in my animal self, in that part of me that breathes fresh air and feels the raw earth between my toes. Yes, the world is as harsh as it is beautiful, but that only brings the wonder of it into sharper relief. Yes, I have issues with black flies, poison ivy, leeches, spiders and the kind of microbes that eat flesh, but they are no less alive than I am. Maybe someday I will learn to accept them for what they are. Maybe, in due time, I will accept the unpleasant aspects of nature along with its pleasant ones, even as I try to make the world a better place.

Unmasking the Laws of Nature

Does nature exist apart from our idea of it? For as long as we have been using the word "nature," we have assumed that there is a certain order to things, that immutable laws rule the universe. Logic dictates that a Supreme Being once created those laws, or that they have always existed. Either way, nature *is* its laws. Nature with a capital "N" that is – nature as a recognizable fabric, as an indivisible whole. But all this is highly speculative. Nature, defined even in this the simplest of terms, still remains a profound assumption embraced by religious and secular minds alike. Who's to say that chaos doesn't rule the universe? How can we be sure that what we call nature isn't an illusion?

Newton's Universal Law of Gravity not only marked the final triumph of Copernican's sun-centered worldview over ancient and medieval fallacies, it ushered in a whole new way of thinking, predicated upon the belief that all nature operates according to unvarying mathematical laws. The Age of Enlightenment began with this fundamental concept. With the acceptance of Newton's gravitational law, scientific method emerged in the late 17[h] Century as the best possible way to solve problems and promote technological innovation. And today it remains the dominant paradigm. The days of the shaman are behind us. It's all about science now. The laws of nature, created by God or no, rule the world in which we live. Or so we tell ourselves.

In the first part of the 19th Century, Ralph Waldo Emerson voiced a radically new worldview that, in retrospect, seems perfectly in tune with the spirit of his time. He believed that religion could be served by science, that God's will is manifest in the laws of nature. He also believed that nature was emblematic of a greater reality, and that we could better understand these "higher laws" through direct encounter with nature. "The foregoing generations beheld God and nature face to face," he wrote in his slender volume called *Nature,* "Why should not we also enjoy an original relation to the universe?" At first Emerson was heavily criticized for his somewhat pantheist views, but soon it became evident that science was leaving traditional religion in the dust. Linnaeus, Herschel, Hooker, Darwin and other scientific heavyweights of the time were fleshing out the laws of nature with such vigor that a new religion was needed to keep pace. Emerson understood this, as did those preaching similar worldviews.

While it was common for 19th Century theologians and philosophers to argue among themselves about whether or not a Supreme Being generated the laws of nature, every scientist hard at work in those days assumed that such laws do exist. Some of them harbored deeply religious convictions; others did not. No matter. Science advanced regardless. But all this changed in the early part of the 20th Century, when the laws of nature were suddenly brought into question by two major breakthroughs in the field of physics: Einstein's Theory of Relativity and the emergence of quantum mechanics. Then the religious and philosophical assumptions behind the word "nature" rose to the forefront.

As far back as the 5th Century B.C., a handful of Greek philosophers cultivated sophisticated theories about the fundamental stuff of nature. The four basic elements – fire, water, earth and sky – dominated popular belief at that time, but a thinker named Democritus saw things differently. Democritus was the first philosopher to see atoms as the building blocks of matter and to differentiate them from empty space. Over the centuries that followed, this notion was forgotten. During the Dark Ages, little thought was given to *how* God created the world. All that mattered was that He did. So the concept of atoms vanished, along with any real interest in physics. But when Copernicus, Kepler, Newton and their kind started probing deeply into the way the universe works, the fundamental stuff of nature was back in the picture. By the beginning of the 20th Century, theoretical physics had returned with a vengeance.

Einstein's Theory of Relativity challenged the classic physics of Isaac Newton. His Special Theory, first published in 1905 in a paper called "On the Electrodynamics of Moving Bodies," showed that things are never quite as they seem. Expanded a decade later into the General Theory of Relativity, Einstein's physics dismissed the existence of absolute time and absolute space, replacing them both with a fourth dimension called *spacetime*. Astronomical observations made by Arthur Stanley Eddington and others in 1919 lent credence to this view. During a solar eclipse, they noticed that stars near the Sun weren't exactly where they were supposed to be, thus proving that light bends just as Einstein's theory predicted. If light bends, then space is curved. That means straight lines do not actually exist. That means the world as we've known it since Euclid invented geometry thousands of years ago is an illusion for the most part. Clearly the Theory of Relativity was a body blow to the so-called laws of nature. If we can't trust our perception of the world, what can we trust?

About the same time that Einstein was working up theories explaining nature on the cosmic scale, other physicists were looking the opposite direction, studying nature at the very smallest level. Not only did they prove the existence of atoms theorized by Democritus long ago, but they identified subatomic particles constituting those atoms, as well. In fact, their discoveries put an end to our conventional understanding of nature. The particles they found – or packets of energy as they were also described – are more basic than time, space and matter themselves. Werner Heisenberg slam-dunked this concept with his Uncertainty Principle. Simply put, Heisenberg's principle states that we can know the speed of a particle or its location in space but not both at the same time. This means that nature, at least at the subatomic level, is dominated by random occurrences – quantum leaps in space and time. And that idea altered the laws of nature forever.

Even though Einstein had shattered the classic laws of Newtonian physics with his own theories, he didn't particularly like the unruly implications of quantum mechanics. "God does not play dice," he asserted, still believing that immutable laws still reign supreme in the universe. Relativity affirmed cosmic order, or so Einstein assured us. Unfortunately, quantum mechanics did not. The result was a profound discrepancy between the macro-world of relativity and the micro-world of quantum mechanics. It's a discrepancy that still haunts us today.

No self-respecting physicist could leave such a discrepancy alone. During the last thirty years of his life, Einstein tried to combine the basic forces of the universe – electro-magnetism, gravity, weak and strong nuclear forces – into one primeval force explained by a Grand Unified Theory. Only then could Relativity hold up to the challenge of quantum mechanics. But he came up empty-handed. Since his death, the best scientific minds in the world have been hard at work on this problem.

One of the brightest physicists of our time, Stephen Hawking, has been trying for decades to fuse Relativity with quantum mechanics to create a Theory of Everything. Hawking is convinced, as many physicists are, that devising some concept of *quantum gravity* is the key to solving the discrepancy. Gravity is, after all, the linchpin of Einstein's Theory of Relativity. As a consequence, Hawking has delved deep into the physics of black holes – those cosmic anomalies in deep space that defy all logic. Black holes are centers of runaway gravitational collapse located throughout the universe. Black holes are where the infinitely large and the infinitely small meet, where huge stars have collapsed to unimaginably small, dense points. Here our conventional notions of space, time and matter break down. "Such a point is an example of what mathematicians call a singularity," Hawking says. But the word "singularity" is very dangerous. Like the word "infinity," it smacks more of mysticism than any scientist is willing to admit.

The advocates of String Theory are taking the discussion to the next level. The laws of nature, it seems, aren't dead after all – they're merely being reinvented. Now there is talk of ten dimensions or more, multi-verses, and infinitesimally small bits of information organizing and reorganizing into strings that form the material universe. Science is still predicated upon immutable laws, these new theorists tell us. No need to worry about that. And the word "nature" still signifies something. Or so they say. But the theories keep getting stranger and more elaborate.

When it comes to the laws of nature, I believe Emerson was right all along. It's easy nowadays to dismiss his quaint essays as the romantic notions of a nature-loving Yankee a century and a half behind the times, but we are gradually reaching the same conclusion he did, that nature is emblematic of a higher reality. The world as it is commonly known is but an illusion. Now that we finally have the courage to look beyond mere appearances, we are discovering metaphysical principles stranger than anything a Neolithic shaman could have dreamed up. And this, no doubt, is just the beginning.

We've come a long way since the days when Copernicus first proposed his sun-centered worldview. That was five hundred years ago. God only knows where we'll be five hundred years from now. The laws of nature keep changing. At times they seem as far beyond our grasp as absolute knowledge, but we keep trying to understand them.

At some point during the past century, we crossed the invisible frontier of logic. Now we are layering abstractions upon abstractions. As Banesh Hoffmann wrote in *The Strange Story of the Quantum*, "It is difficult to decide where science ends and mysticism begins." The minute we trained our tools upon the fundamental forces of nature and started thinking deeply about how they operate, we ventured down that long and twisting road leading into the nebulous realm of metaphysics. The Higgs boson is often referred to as "the God particle" by physicists and for good reason. Theoretically, that particle gives all material things their mass. I am tempted to genuflect or at least make the sign of the cross whenever someone mentions it. This kind of science is very close to being religion. It is fraught with philosophical assumptions, to say the least.

The natural world operates according to certain immutable laws. We have to believe this. If chaos reigns in the universe and everything around us is merely happenstance, then what's the point of thinking at all? In that case, we would be better off abandoning both religion and science, giving up all pretence of ever knowing the world, and go back to living moment-to-moment as other creatures do. But we're beyond that now, aren't we? The fact that we think suggests that we have something worth thinking about. When one considers how successfully our species has manipulated nature over the millennia through the power of abstract thought, it is easy to believe that we should continue operating this way. And who knows? Maybe someday we will unmask the laws of nature once and for all.

The Impossible Cosmos

The truth of the world is written in the stars. Shamans believed as much in the centuries before the birth of civilizations, and later high priests acted upon this belief. They built temples in alignment with the sky, calibrating the positions of the sun, moon and stars, thus divining the mysterious ways of the gods. They marked time, creating the calendars that became invaluable aids for planting, harvesting and other agricultural practices. But eventually the hunger for truth drove them to look deeper still, until disturbing facts about the world emerged. Then they recoiled from the glittery sky, closing their minds. Centuries passed. When finally rational thinkers looked skyward, certain cosmic realities became inescapable. Then the relationship between humankind and the universe at large changed forever.

Ever since I was a kid, I have looked to the stars with burning curiosity. First I looked at them with naked eyes, then with binoculars and telescopes. I have read books about them, as well. As the decades have gone by, my interest in astronomy has grown. But I didn't delve deeply into the subject until a few years ago. Not until I was surfing the Internet, ogling the celestial phenomenon on display at various websites, did my interest in the night sky grow beyond the casual. That's when I stumbled upon a site run by the U.S. government that stated rather matter-of-factly: "This year, humanity learned that the universe is

13.7 billion years old." That lofty proclamation got my attention. I didn't automatically accept it, but it got my attention all the same.

For as long as I can remember, astrophysicists have been arguing about whether the universe has always existed in a "steady state" similar to what we see today, or was the result of some immeasurably great cosmological event. That event, commonly referred to as the Big Bang, is an assumption embraced by all those who think that the universe has changed fundamentally over time. For as long as I've been alive, the Big Bang has been a theory and a theory only – one of several entertained by astrophysicists. To actually fix a date to the Big Bang, well, that goes beyond assumption. When did this theory become a fact?

For as long as I can remember, believers in the Big Bang have been hotly debating when that great cosmological event occurred. Dates have varied wildly between 10 and 20 billion years ago. For decades I have half-listened to these speculations, shrugging them off as only so much sloppy guesswork. Then suddenly we are told that the universe is 13.7 billion years old. Never before has anyone had the audacity to use a decimal point, or to make a statement about the age of the universe as if its having a birth date was a given. So I looked into the matter.

The website in question, Astronomy Picture of the Day, highlighted the findings of the Wilkinson Microwave Anisotropy Probe (WMAP) launched in the spring of 2003. That probe measured the Cosmic Microwave Background (CMB) of the entire universe. Evidently, the radiation left over from the Big Bang is measurable. In the early 1990s, a similar instrument called the Cosmic Background Explorer (COBE) was sent into space. But WMAP has provided us with much more detailed information regarding CMB. Together these satellites, along with data derived from supernovas, have brought about the demise of the Steady State Theory of the universe. Many 20th Century scientists, including Einstein, favored the Steady State Theory. But now, it seems, the Big Bang is the only game in town.

Now we are told that the Big Bang Theory is no longer a theory at all. It's a simple fact. I am incensed by this proclamation. I want to deny it. I want the details laid in front of me, at least, so that I can make my own assessment. So *this* is how the Church scholars must have felt in the early 1600s when they read Galileo's book. Believing is easy, and speculating about the nature of the universe is fun, but accepting some statement about the cosmos as a given, well, that's another thing altogether. Even though I have always *believed* in the Big Bang, I find it difficult to accept as an irrefutable fact.

In the 1920s, about the same time that quantum mechanics and relativity were coming to light, the American astronomer Edwin Hubble showed that the universe is expanding. Hubble never embraced any particular theory of the universe. He was a scientist, a meticulous observer of things, interested only in the facts. As far back as 1885, astronomers had noticed conspicuously bright stars in Andromeda and other faraway nebulae. The light emitted by those stars varies over time. In fact, these variances of illumination are both regular and predictable. Because of this, Hubble and his associates were able to use variable stars to determine the distance between our own Milky Way and faraway nebulae such as Andromeda. Two important scientific breakthroughs occurred as a result. First, we learned that those faraway nebulae are galaxies unto themselves – similar to yet completely separate from our own Milky Way. Second, we learned that, with the exception of Andromeda and a few other galaxies that are relatively close, all other galaxies are moving away from us. In other words, the universe is expanding.

A French priest and astronomer named Georges Lemaître was the first to give Hubble's observations their distinctly religious overtone. An expanding universe implies that the universe once had a beginning. This is reminiscent of the first few lines of the Bible: "In the beginning God created the heavens..." and all that. Consequently, the word "beginning" has rubbed many scientists the wrong way. "Philosophically," Arthur Eddington wrote, "The notion of a beginning of the present order of nature is repugnant to me." He was not alone.

In the middle of the 20th Century, two notable scientists, George Gamow and Fred Hoyle, publicly debated the matter – Gamow arguing in favor of the Big Bang and Hoyle against. It was Hoyle, in fact, who coined the term "Big Bang." He used the term disparagingly in a radio show in 1949. Shortly thereafter, he wrote: "The big bang idea seemed to me unsatisfactory even before detailed examination showed that it leads to serious difficulties." Serious difficulties, indeed. To a believer in the Steady State Theory, it was the scientific equivalent of heresy.

Time and space go hand in hand. Those who ponder the nature of the universe eventually come around to this conclusion, it seems. The Jewish theologian Moses Maimonides reached it back in the 12th Century when he said: "If you admit the existence of time before the creation, you will be compelled to accept the theory of the eternity of the universe." It's hard to refute the logic of this statement. So it can't be helped: science and religion are bound to step on each other's toes. It's inevitable. It's inevitable because physics becomes metaphysics the moment that a religious proclamation or a scientific observation infers anything about time, space, or the universe at large. God-talk and cosmology are one in the same.

Rene Descartes, the patron saint of reason, reopened that cosmological can of worms in the middle of the 17th Century when he wrote: "By the name God, I understand a substance infinite." Plato and Aristotle had addressed this matter 2,500 years earlier, taking diametrically opposed stances. Plato argued a Self-moved Mover; Aristotle an Unmoved Mover. In other words, either God is an integral part of the universe or He stands outside of it as its Creator. Either way, *something* must be infinite. One could say that Gamow with his "big bang" worldview and Hoyle with his "steady state" universe took up positions mimicking those held by the two ancient Greek philosophers. The word "infinite" is the source of all our troubles here. It's not difficult to see why.

There are rumors of folks pondering infinity to the point of insanity. Theologians, mathematicians and astronomers run the greatest risk of being consumed by this madness, no doubt. At some point, it is best to simply shake one's head then say "This is what I believe," and leave it at that. Trying to get to the bottom of things may be an exercise in futility – the dog chasing its tail. The word "infinity" torments the logic-driven mind. It refers to something clearly beyond comprehension. We can say that the universe has roughly 100 billion galaxies in it, each with 100 billion stars more or less, and we can almost grasp that. But to say it's *infinite*, well, that overloads our brains and effectively shuts down the conversation. Curiously enough, the word "infinity" surfaces in every debate about the nature of the universe, if the matter is pursued long enough. It is hardwired into the subject.

While some scientists have been busy investigating the Big Bang, others have made great strides regarding the cosmic expansion that Hubble first observed many decades ago. Along with CMB measurements, observations of supernovas in faraway galaxies have given us vital clues regarding the nature of the universe. Supernovas are massive stars in their death throes. Each supernova emits a sudden burst of incredibly bright light, followed by a gradual fading. Like Hubble's variable stars, supernovas are "standard candles" by which we can measure great speeds and distances. The inference of these recent supernova observations is shocking – just the opposite of what one would expect to find. During the last few billion years, if seems, the universe has not only expanded but has done so at *an ever-increasing rate*. How is this possible?

Naturally, if God created the universe in a Big Bang, then it must end in a similar fashion. God or no, if the universe has expanded to its present state from a singularity – a single point of spacetime, that is – then surely it must collapse back into one, right? The expansion must eventually slow down, come to a halt, and then the universe must start contracting. This only stands to reason. Surely there can be no Creation without an accompanying Apocalypse. But a universe being born, then expanding at an ever-increasing rate with no end in sight – my head explodes at the mere thought of it. Doesn't yours?

Either the universe began and will someday end, or it is infinite. Logic dictates that we make a choice here. Can't have it both ways. P or not P – that is the basis of all rational thought. If the Big Bang is a fact, then an ever-expanding universe is impossible. So what is missing here? What is it that we haven't taken into account?

The natural world is easy to grasp until you really start thinking about it. Trouble begins the moment you turn an eye towards the night sky and speculate. Trouble mounts when you look closely at the very small. Trouble rages when you focus your powerful instruments on both sub-atomic particles and the edge of the visible universe, carefully noting what you find there. The Church's Inquisitors knew exactly what they were doing when they burned Bruno at the stake for espousing that Copernican heresy. Too much information is dangerous and unsettling. People can't go merrily about their day-to-day affairs in an impossible cosmos. The world has to make sense, even if that means filling in the blanks with utter nonsense. The unknown troubles us all.

A careful observer of scientific revolutions, Thomas Kuhn once posed this compelling question: "What is it that transforms an apparently temporary discrepancy into an inescapable conflict?" That's precisely what we dealt with four centuries ago, at the height of the Copernican Revolution, and what we are dealing with again today. A radical shift in thinking is taking place. No one fully understands all the changes currently underway or where they will take us. The only thing we can say for certain is that recent breakthroughs in astronomy and physics are creating "an inescapable conflict" as Kuhn called it. Personally, I believe that science is reinventing religion, that our constant probing deep into space is only intensifying the great mysteries of nature. The more we learn about the universe, the more we realize how much more there is to learn. The unknown still looms large before us – now more than ever.

A hundred years ago, God-talk was close to being removed once and for all from the field of cosmology. But advances in astronomy and physics have muddied the water since then, broadening the scope of the unknown, thus confounding that tidy, "steady state" view of things. Had we looked no farther than Harlow Shapley did back in the early 20th Century, when he declared that the Milky Way *is* the universe, we would not have noticed the expansion. In another place and time, Hubble's observations would have been considered heretical and Lemaître would have been burned at the stake for making too much of it. Not that it would have mattered. As history shows, time and time again, the truth has a way of getting out.

I don't like living in an impossible cosmos but feel I have no choice in the matter. The whole truth about the universe isn't known yet. I'll probably go to my grave before it is. I suspect that the whole truth may never be known. Some integral part of nature and existence will always remain beyond our grasp. But I could be wrong about this. With human capabilities being what they are, it's foolish to make any definitive claims about what can or cannot be known tomorrow.

The Emergence of Life

I nearly choked on my dinner as the lecturer on television displayed colorful images of nebulas on the screen behind him, casually announcing to anyone who would listen that all the building blocks of life existed there. Simple carbon compounds, hydrogen, nitrogen and oxygen – they're all there. He speculated that primitive life forms might even exist in those immense clouds of gas deep in space, that some nebulas are dense enough to screen out the harmful radiation that would otherwise kill such organisms. I immediately checked the television guide to make sure that I hadn't surfed into the Science Fiction channel by mistake. No, this was an educational program on public television and this guy was dead serious. Next thing I knew, I was wondering what constitutes life and how it came to be.

About twenty years ago, when I owned and operated a used bookstore, I stumbled upon a Dover paperback titled *Origin of Life*. Written by a Russian named A. I. Oparin, the book had first been published back in the 1930s. I'd never heard of it before but it looked interesting so I took it home and read it. I scratched my head as the author discussed "spontaneous generation" – a theory popular with the ancient Greeks and taken seriously by scientists as late as the 19th Century. Spontaneous? How do you get something from nothing? Then I laughed out loud when Oparin touched upon the idea entertained by some that the germ of life could have fallen to earth from outer space, in a meteorite or something. All this was a set up, of course.

What that cagey Russian scientist was really trying to show was that life most likely evolved from simple carbon compounds on this planet over long periods of time – over millions, perhaps even billions, of years. Here was the "primeval soup" concept as it is taught to grade school kids today. But Oparin's protracted discourse on the subject made me realize just how difficult the transition must have been, how elaborate the chemistry had to be for even the simplest living organism to emerge from inanimate matter.

Once you have a single-celled organism splitting into two cells, life is off and running. Cells multiply exponentially, taking on different characteristics over time, and eventually the entire planet is covered with organisms, all kinds of organisms, interacting with each other in the complex web of life that we call nature. Evolution adequately explains all this. But how do you get from chemical compounds, however elaborate, to that first organism? How do you transform inanimate matter into something animate? Herein lies one of the greatest mysteries of the universe.

Most people never give the origin of life a second thought. They say that God created life and that's all there is to it. Or they take a more secular point of view, assuming that life emerged from a simple mechanistic process that took place long ago. Those who don't believe in a Creator naturally think that this process will be reproduced in a laboratory someday. Zap a flask full of the right chemicals with a little electricity and voila! Okay, maybe it won't be that easy, but surely the process will be duplicated in due time. All we have to do is work out the details, right?

Going back and rereading Oparin, it occurs to me that it doesn't really matter whether the germ of life emerged on this planet or came here from somewhere else. At some point that germ had to arise from inanimate matter, and *something* had to trigger the transformation. That event marked a sudden and radical change in the universe. A single cell organism, the very first life form, arose from something no more alive than slime in a tidal pool. What could be more astounding?

Life forms are composed of the same elements that constitute inanimate matter, but that isn't all there is to the story. To fully appreciate the emergence of life, one must look at the big picture. What do we actually know about the elements? What do we know about the stuff of the universe at large? Thanks to an eccentric Swiss astrophysicist named Fritz Zwicky, and those who built upon his work, we know that most of the physical universe isn't physical at all – at least not as we commonly think of it. Most of the universe is either dark energy or dark matter. Dark energy is a mysterious kind of anti-gravitational force. Dark matter is probably non-baryonic stuff, though it might include dead stars and other unseen material made up of atoms. "Non-baryonic" means that the substance in question isn't organized into atoms yet. It's just a loose array of subatomic particles – something that may never be organized.

The part of the universe that is physical in the conventional sense of the word consists mostly of hydrogen and helium. All the other elements on the Periodic Table – carbon, nitrogen, oxygen and the like – are byproducts of hydrogen and helium atoms fused together inside heavy stars. Elements other than hydrogen and helium make up only a tiny fraction of the universe – less than one percent, if we take dark energy and dark matter into account. Yet from these elements nature as we know it arises.

Relatively large spiral galaxies, such as Andromeda and the Milky Way, are busy places chock full of gaseous, star-forming nebulas. The material essential for life is forged in the cores of heavy stars once generated by those nebulas. When heavy stars die in immense explosions known as supernovas, the material essential for life is scattered across the galaxy. Eventually, that material coalesces into rocks great and small colliding into each other, thus creating planets. Then the emergence of life is just a matter of time and the right conditions.

What exactly are the right conditions for the emergence of life? Certain temperatures, an atmosphere screening out harmful radiation, sufficient energy from the sun or some other source, the proper mix of chemical compounds, water or some kind of fluid – the list goes on. You aren't going to create life in a vacuum tube as some scientists had hoped a hundred years ago. The process is much more complex, contingent upon many factors. Life is, above all else, *involved.*

I think the naturalist John Burroughs got it right when he said: "Life is so great a mystery that we need not invent others." No force in nature is as remarkable as that which transforms the inanimate into the animate. Life forms are born then die everywhere around us all the time. We do the same. Yet no one can explain how the even the simplest organism can spring from inanimate matter then return to it. An egg is fertilized by sperm, then one cell becomes two, then four, and on and on like that until suddenly a baby pops from a mother's womb and gasps for air. In due time, its heart stops, all systems fail, and what was a philosopher, caregiver, businessman or athlete is now only so much decaying flesh – material ready to be recycled. How is it that we can launch probes deep into space, split the atom, and transform wafers of silicon into vast banks of information yet know so little about something as fundamental as life?

Mother Nature jealously guards her secrets. She keeps us in the dark about that which matters most. As Ursula Goodenough wrote in *The Sacred Depths of Nature*, "Mystery generates wonder, and wonder generates awe." And we are left with that. Whatever causes life, how the inanimate becomes animate, remains beyond our comprehension. We are acutely aware of the process – how complex protein sequences are built, how DNA scripts various life forms – yet no wiser for it. We are dumbfounded by the existence of the simplest organisms, by all livings things, by our own existence. Why are we here? How did we get here? The answers to these questions are only so much wild conjecture.

The details we know for the most part – from supernova to carbon compounds, or from a replicating single-celled creature to us – but that great leap between the inanimate and the animate still stumps us. Someday we may close this gap in our knowledge. Yeah, maybe someday we'll know all of the details. But will we ever know what life is exactly or why it exists?

We are stardust – that much is certain. When God made Adam, he took a handful of earth and breathed life into it, or so the story goes. That story isn't too far off the mark. Astrophysical, geophysical, and chemical facts prove that we are connected to the earth beneath our feet and the stars overhead. But our existence is no less remarkable because of these facts. Our existence is no less a mystery because we can show that we are made of the same elements as everything else. That's precisely what makes it so amazing.

A Web of Complex Relations

Although living things constitute a mere fraction of the physical universe, they are what most people have in mind when they think about nature. The inanimate is only the backdrop for the animate, it seems. It is the business of living that interests us most. This was no less true for that 19th Century naturalist, Charles Darwin, who so radically changed the way we look at the world. He focused on living things, studied them in depth, and constructed his theory of nature accordingly. His theory is based upon the animate, not the inanimate, so it quickly stirred everyone's blood. Even today, it is still hotly debated.

The word "Darwinism" implies all sorts of assumptions about the world – assumptions that were embraced by Darwin and assumptions that were not. As with all great teachings, the core message is often lost in the cacophony of interpretations that follows. The theory that Darwin espoused a hundred and fifty years ago has now taken on a life of its own. There are those who profess to be Darwinists who have never read a line of Darwin's work. Yet the kernel of his worldview is still there in the writing left behind for anyone willing to take the time to look.

Darwin wasn't the first person to suggest that plants and animals undergo profound changes over great periods of time. In the "historical sketch" that he added to *The Origin of Species*, he gave due credit to Lamarck, Saint-Hilaire, and a host of other scientists, naturalists and philosophers who entertained the idea of evolution during the latter part of the 18th Century the first half of the 19th. It was, to some extent, an idea whose time had come. Though he believed his work was incomplete, Darwin rushed his famous theory into publication in 1859, shortly after a scientist named Alfred Wallace published a paper on the subject. In that day, the wealth of data that Darwin and others had collected was making the theory of evolution a foregone conclusion among those scientists willing to look beyond a strictly *religious* view of nature. All that remained was to articulate these findings to skeptics like the renowned naturalist Louis Agassiz, and the public at large. Or so they thought.

New varieties of plants can emerge from old ones – this is an obvious fact to anyone who works with them. Those who devote their lives to horticultural practices see this kind of change all the time. Human beings have been cross-fertilizing plants and creating new ones for thousands of years. We've been crossbreeding animals, as well. And no one is surprised by the results. But to say that plants and animals can change on their own, mutating over time into completely new species, well, that's another matter altogether. In the mid-19th Century, this concept was revolutionary.

The natural world is fecund. Life has not only insinuated itself into an inanimate universe, but is constantly asserting itself. Everywhere you look, plants and animals reproduce at a frenzied pace. And they devour each other in the process – the consumption of organic matter being essential to the survival of countless life forms. As Darwin wrote in *The Origin of Species*, "A struggle for existence inevitably follows from the high rate at which all organic beings tend to increase." This struggle is taking place right before our

51

eyes. It is the basis of all change in plants and animals. It is an irresistible force.

Plants suck minerals from the earth and, with the help of sunlight, create the sugars that are essential to their existence. Herbivores eat those plants, and carnivores eat the herbivores. Microbes eat whatever they can. Parasites attach themselves to plants and animals alike. Some organisms work together. Lichen, for example, is the symbiotic relationship between algae and fungi. For others, like wolves and moose, life is a zero-sum game. Strategies vary but the goal remains the same for all life forms: to exist, to reproduce, to perpetuate one's own kind even if it means changing into something slightly different in the process. Look around and you'll see it. The consequences of this struggle are clearly apparent everywhere. Wild nature revels in it. Life is raging. It runs amok in the world. It is a force operating beyond the control of any governing body, natural or otherwise.

The English philosopher Herbert Spencer is the one who coined the term "survival of the fittest," thus giving Darwinism its *social* implications. Darwin himself used the term "natural selection" when he first wrote about the ways of wild nature. A careful reading of *The Origin of Species* shows why. While most "Social Darwinists" believe that ours is a dog-eat-dog world, Darwin himself always emphasized the role of adaptation. The most powerful forces at work in the natural world are reproductive. Variation is the great evolutionary driver, not tooth and claw. It's all about change in nature, not conquest, and this change occurs genetically in response to environmental circumstances. Many interpreters of Darwin's theory miss this point altogether. Either that or they ignore it.

Darwin studied the relationships between one life form and another, between varying individuals, between different species of plants and animals, between all living things. He believed that all plants and animals, even the smallest and seemingly insignificant, "are bound together by a web of complex relations." To some Darwinists, that web *is* wild nature. But I would extend the web to all things, both living and non-living. It's absurd to talk about any of the particulars of nature without taking into consideration nature as a whole. It's absurd to look at life forms while ignoring the inanimate matter with which they interact. The wind, rain, and earth influence the lily, tiger, and the butterfly. All things are connected.

Order and chaos. At times it seems like nature has achieved balance, then some cataclysmic event occurs. We want to believe that all creatures great and small can live in harmony, that the wild song of nature has reached a perfect pitch and any deviation will only diminish it. But that's not the case. Great plagues break out, storms rage, drought ensue, crops fail, and things are pretty much the way they've always been. But we assume that something has gone terribly wrong. Somehow we have provoked the gods and must now make amends. We suffer the plagues, droughts and floods, hoping that things will get back to normal soon. But "normal" is only how we perceive things on the short run. It isn't reality. The violent disruptions that occur periodically are simply nature being itself. In the greater scheme of things, they are common enough. Sometimes Mother Nature is benign; other times she is not. As difficult as it is for us to accept, chaos and disruption are as much a part of nature as order and balance.

What's the difference between a perverse mutation and an evolutionary advance? Whether it persists or not, that's all. Successful life forms find a place for themselves in the world. Unsuccessful ones do not. That's all there is to it.

There's really no reason to believe that the natural world *ought* to be this particular way or that. Nature simply is. And the life forms in it either persist or they don't. Words like "right" or "wrong" have no place in the wild.

Natural scientists cling to their immutable laws. They worship a universe ruled by mathematics. Those more religiously inclined have God's plan, or whatever grand design they believe is driving the world. But nothing in wild nature exists without exception. There is no order without chaos. As vexing as it may seem to us, wild nature has no agenda. It follows no blueprint or design known to humankind. It simply persists.

"Introduce design into nature and you humanize it and get into difficulties at once," John Burroughs once wrote, "It is above design." The wild proves this point time and again. We have a hard time accepting this. We want the world to function according to intelligible rules, either secular or religious. We want the universe to make sense, always, without exception, beyond all reasonable doubt. But that's not how things are. Subatomic particles bounce around haphazardly, the universe expands, our planet convulses, and the countless life forms around us are constantly changing. Everything is in flux. It's a wild ride and all we can do is hang on. Whatever God's intentions are – God being defined here as the organizing force of the universe – they are clearly beyond any *human* understanding. Burroughs was right, I think. The word "design" doesn't adequately describe what nature is all about. By definition the wild is something unpredictable, something beyond control.

In a sense, natural selection is one of the most profoundly religious notions ever postulated. It lends order to nature without limiting things. Written into the mechanics of evolution is the presumption that some organizing force is at work in the world, that all of wild nature is compelled towards some end, and that life – a relative newcomer in the universe – perpetuates itself. Yet the *reason* for that perpetuation remains beyond us. Clearly the ways of wild nature and the ways of humankind are two different things.

The ongoing fight nowadays between Darwinists and Creationists is absurd, I think. Here are two blind men giving different descriptions of the same elephant, as the saying goes. Nature, if it exists at all, must have some kind of order to it. But there is always room for surprise. In nature, the "under construction" sign is never taken away. The wonder of wild nature is that there's room enough for both order *and* chaos. Nowhere is this more evident than in the fossil record etched into the earth. The wild has invented every kind of life form imaginable and then some. And it's not finished yet.

"The universe endures," the evolutionist philosopher Henry Bergson once said. In the passage of time he saw the unfolding of new forms, "the continual elaboration of the absolutely new." How could the world be otherwise? The universe is constantly on the move, along with everything in it. Nature is a web of relations so intricate, so complex, that it can't help but change.

The wild reigns supreme, and there are times when it seems like anything goes. Yet a fabric exists – a perceptible order shining through an apparently random series of events. Evolution, now much more than mere theory, suggests that organizing forces are hard at work in the world. Nature evolves and some semblance of order is evident in the process even if we can't fully grasp it. Everything changes, certainly, but all is not chaos.

On Being Human

Human beings are a part of nature. We eat, sleep, and reproduce like all other animals. We are susceptible to temperature extremes, need air to breathe, and bleed when we are cut. Most importantly, we are born and eventually die. In these and more subtle ways we are bound to the earth – just another strand in that web of complex relations better known as the natural world. Yet there is something different about us, something that sets us apart from the rest of existence. Someday the other animals may argue that there is no basis whatsoever for this elitist attitude of ours. But until they do, we will assume it. Hence the question arises: What makes us different?

In the 20th Century, a relatively obscure religious philosopher named Abraham J. Heschel posed the compelling question: "Who is Man?" then attempted to answer it. "Who?' he asked, not "What?" as if identity was the key to understanding ourselves, not attributes. Heschel's conclusion was that "he is a being who asks questions concerning himself." This answer comes dangerously close to saying nothing at all, like that famous Cartesian dictum: "I think therefore I am." Yet herein lies the crux of the matter. While it is true that we don't know what a frog, a bird or a bear is thinking, it's clear that the mere act of asking questions has changed us in profound ways. Asking any question whatsoever indicates a level of awareness that is bound to change the creature asking it. Asking a question regarding one's identity takes this to the next level. Self-awareness is the beginning of heightened awareness and must weigh heavily in any meaningful definition of the human. Other creatures may think to some greater or lesser extent, but we do it like no others. Our tremendous impact upon the world is proof of that.

A few million years ago, a small hominid walked upright across the African savanna. Until it came along, primates were creatures of the trees for the most part. Walking upright changed all that. It opened up the rest of the world. Walking upright – being a true biped, that is – isn't as easy as it sounds. It takes more than merely being able to lumber about on hind legs for short distances. It requires significant changes in skeletal structure. This indicates a radical change in survival strategy, resulting almost immediately – immediate by evolutionary standards – in a head larger in proportion to the body than those sported by other animals. More room was needed to accommodate the extra brain functions demanded by upright locomotion, among other things. Here we have our most distant ancestor, *Australopithecus*. Mary Leakey made this creature famous a half century ago when she found its bones in eastern Africa. And now scientists believe that *Australopithecus* satisfies most of the "missing link" criteria that connect us to the rest of the animal kingdom. Most criteria, but certainly not all of them.

Our genus, *Homo*, arrived on the scene about a million years later. *Homo habilis* is one of the names given to the earliest humanlike creatures. "Habilis" refers to the ability to make simple stone tools. Call this guy "Handy Man" and you're not far off the mark. Nowadays most scientists place this creature in the larger category *Homo erectus* – a hominid walking erect whose survival strategies kept it going well over a half million years. The brain case of *Homo erectus* grew by leaps and bounds during that time, practically doubling in size. Here's a big clue as to who or what we are.

Archaic humans, the very first *Homo sapiens*, appeared in the world just as *Homo erectus* was fading away. Archaic humans took tool making to a whole new level. From this distant ancestor both Neanderthals and modern humans emerged. The former was a successful hunter during the Ice Age who lost his competitive edge when the climate changed. The modern human, on the other hand, sported a massive frontal lobe and the uncanny ability to adapt to rapidly changing conditions. Do we dare posit a connection between that frontal lobe – the center of both emotion and higher reasoning functions – and our ability to prevail? I don't think that's too much of a stretch.

Modern humans – yes, that's us. We are *Homo sapiens sapiens*, translating loosely to "Man Who Really Knows." Since we're the ones digging up our distant ancestors and naming them, it only makes sense that we'd flatter ourselves with such a lofty title. But there is more to this than mere egotism. Our brains are proportionally larger than those of any other hominid that has ever roamed the earth, with the possible exception of our poor cousins the Neanderthals. We are the eggheads of nature, and our remarkable success since the demise of the Neanderthals suggests that we deserve the title. We are nearly seven billion strong now and still multiplying. No other hominid has ever come close to this kind of success. For all practical purposes, we have taken over the planet. One would be hard-pressed to find a square mile of earth, water or sky where we haven't left our mark.

What qualities do we possess that are unique? Opposable thumbs are common among primates, walking upright was around long before humanity, and chimps can use sticks as tools to extract termites from mounds. No, physically there's not much unique about us at all. Only our brains separate us in any significant way from the rest of creation. We have the ability to think abstractly – a skill that goes hand-in-hand with acute self-awareness. That's the main thing.

Abstraction has made us what we are today. We started burying our dead many thousands of years ago – a ritual showing a strong inclination towards abstraction. We speak in languages fraught with symbolism – yet another feature suggesting that we've been thinking abstractly for a long time. The pictures left behind on cave walls by our distant ancestors are further proof of this. Above all else, our abstract thoughts are written in stone, in the difference between our tools and the tools of those who came before us. About 50,000 years ago, we underwent a cultural revolution that left our cousins, the Neanderthals, in the dust. We succeeded technologically where they failed. Now they are gone and we have moved into every corner of the earth.

Abstraction, along with the arts and sciences associated with it, has led to human culture in all its forms. "I think therefore I am," Descartes once said, but the change that occurred 50,000 years ago was much more profound than that. Not only did *Homo sapiens* start thinking, therefore becoming acutely aware of "I," it soon realized that some other creature could be an "I" as well – that the world is full of them, that "You" and "We" exist. Therein lies the basis of all advanced culture. Here's a quality well beyond anything the world had seen before we came along.

"Man is nothing else but what he makes of himself," the French philosopher Jean-Paul Sartre wrote in the middle of the last century. This statement is underscored by the ongoing discoveries of paleontologists. Over the millennia, we have made countless tools that have molded the world to our purposes. We have expanded culture and thereby ourselves as a consequence. We are animals, certainly, subject to the same bodily functions as all other animals. And, as individuals, we remain surprisingly vulnerable to nature's ways. But collectively we've done remarkably well for ourselves.

With the freedom that arises from both abstract thought and self-awareness, there comes the ability to choose. As children, we believe what are told to believe. But as we grow older, we develop the ability to think for ourselves. All good and evil stems from this, so thinking abstractly is a prospect as terrifying as it is promising. Different people respond to this challenge in different ways. Some take full responsibility for their actions; others do not. Nonetheless, we all have within us the ability to choose, to determine our destinies to some extent. That much is written in our genes.

Human nature is a subset of nature, yet it remains something separate from the rest of existence. This is the fundamental paradox of being human. There are those who see in humankind only those attributes common to all animals. But they are only seeing what they want to see. There are others who believe that we are godlike beings confined temporarily to mortal bodies. This only goes to show how imaginative the human mind can be. It is easy to see why most people embrace one or the other of these two opposing views. It simply doesn't make sense that we could be both animal and god, both finite and free. That would make us something incomprehensible. Am I, *Homo sapiens*, a walking contradiction, an impossible creature?

The philosopher Susanne K. Langer believed that symbols play a critical role in our perception of the world. In her seminal work, *Philosophy in a New Key*, she argued that

60

symbolization – the direct consequence of our abstractions – is "the keynote of all humanistic problems." To her it didn't matter whether those symbols are practical, mathematical or mystical. The world we have created for ourselves is the consequence of them. So it must be true, as Sartre said, that we are what we make of ourselves.

Sometimes I am inclined to believe that I'm just a link in a Great Chain of Being, that my thoughts and actions are not my own, that my fate was determined long before I was born. Then I make a decision, choosing between two radically divergent courses of action. That's when I begin to think of myself as a god. That is when it occurs to me that I am capable of shaping my own destiny. Such freedom!

Mere animal or godlike? To what extent am I both? It's hard to say which characteristic is stronger. There's no unassailable definition of the human. Like the rest of my kind, I have these complex mental functions whirling in my head that I don't fully understand. No doubt these thoughts define me more than anything else. But is that all there is to being human? I'd have to chat with a Neanderthal or some other extinct hominid for a while in order to determine that.

Civil Inclinations

Few people think much about what it means to be civilized. Assumptions abound, of course. We assume that the technological and cultural advances making our lives easier also make us better people – that the barbarians of the past were not only rough around the edges but not quite as humane as we are. Or we take the opposite view, articulated by the French philosopher Jean Jacques Rousseau in the 18th Century, that we moderns have fallen from grace and that our primitive ancestors were better, more virtuous creatures than us. Built into both of these views is the fundamental assumption that being wild is either a good or a bad thing, and that being civilized ought to be judged accordingly.

Is this true? Is wildness the opposite of civilization? Moreover, can we expect a day to come when the entire planet will be civilized and the word "wild" lose all meaning? Will the wild be wiped out someday, both within us and across the planet, once and for all? Most people would say yes, if we keep to the course we're now following. Some would say this is inevitable. The logic of the prevailing wild-versus-civilized worldview infers it. But I suspect that we've got the idea of wildness all wrong here, and that our civil inclinations do not serve us as well as we think they do.

Many thousands of years ago, our ancestors were painting the walls of caves, engaging in ritualistic practices, and making relatively sophisticated tools. If we apply the word "culture" to what they were doing, then surely civilization must be something else. We all know how the great leap occurred. The rise of civilization was the consequence of agriculture – the large-scale production of food. While still living in the highlands, Neolithic peoples domesticated plants and animals, but not until they moved down into the river valleys did these practices flourish. All this happened somewhere between 5,000 to 10,000 years ago. By 3,000 BC, "cradles of civilization" were firmly established along the Yangtze, Nile, and Indus rivers, as well as the Tigris-Euphrates. Shortly thereafter, civilizations arose in the Americas as well.

The large-scale production of food created surpluses, which led to the formation of towns full of artisans, merchants, and other specialists. The division of labor, commonly found in all urban centers, is the hallmark of civilization. Different people started making different things: clay pots, wheeled carts, boats, and a wide assortment of tools. Animals were put to work in the fields. Textiles were woven and the arts flourished. Metallurgy commenced with the forging of tin and copper to make bronze. Villages grew into towns and towns grew into cities. At first these towns were walled simply to keep out wild animals and brigands, but eventually the walls grew taller and more formidable as territorial disputes between neighbors broke out. For the most part, it was a period of rapidly expanding commerce and cooperation. And humanity as a whole was better off because of it. The steady increase in population that occurred during these centuries confirms this.

With civilization, though, came government. As Elman Service explained in his book, *Origins of the State and Civilization*, simple societies are small and larger ones are more complex. With greater complexity comes social stratification: those in charge, those enforcing their will, and those doing all the work. Priest-kings called the shots in the earliest civilizations, but that changed soon enough. Powerful warlords eventually replaced priest-kings. Then things got ugly. Sargon I of the Akkadians was one of the first of these rulers to take warfare to the next level. In the 23rd Century BC, he put together one of the world's first professional armies – if not *the* first – then systematically conquered Mesopotamia. Humankind has been fighting wars of conquest ever since.

With conquest came the institution of slavery. When one group of people conquers another, the vanquished usually become their slaves. Slaves do the dirty work. That's what they're for. The Egyptian pharaohs used slaves to build pyramids – those magnificent monuments to godlike power. From Roman galleys to American plantations, slavery has persisted throughout the millennia. As recently as the mid-20th Century, totalitarian regimes manned their factories with slave labor. In fact, the Nazi slave system operated with a cold-blooded efficiency that would have greatly impressed the pharaohs. Now that's progress! Various forms of social and economic slavery still exist today. The practice is common throughout the newly industrializing countries where sweatshops prevail. Humankind has perfected the institution of slavery, it seems. Shackles are no longer necessary. Now people can be enslaved by the mere wave of a dollar bill.

Commerce or conflict? Cooperation or conquest? What is the true nature of civilization, and is it really in the best interest of all parties involved? These questions are fodder for endless debate. I wouldn't presume to know the answers. All I can say for certain is this: there are more people alive now than ever before. In general they live longer, healthier lives than their distant ancestors. And

64

there are a host of amenities and conveniences available these days that make modern living quite pleasant, indeed. But the benefits of civilization are not distributed equally. Far from it. As thinkers like Karl Marx have been pointing out for quite some time now, a wealthy few enjoy most of the benefits of civilization while the vast majority of people live barely above the subsistence level, if that. The ways of the pharaohs, it seems, are still with us.

As a college student, I was mystified by the sheer elegance of Martin Buber's philosophy of relationships. In his book, *I and Thou,* he wrote: "One basic word is the word pair I-You. The other basic word is the word pair I-It." The mechanics of human interaction don't get any more basic than that. Either we treat other human beings as if they are persons just like us, or we objectify them. This is the choice we all make. But some people cloud this simple fact with elaborate worldviews that provide the justifications necessary to exploit others. They are quick to enumerate the many reasons why some people deserve more wealth than others, why a privileged few should wield power over everyone else. In the capitalist model, hard work is rewarded and the cream of society rises to the top, or so we are told. In the socialist model, devised by Marx, Engels and their disciples, a select few take charge because they know better than the workers do what's good for them. This "dictatorship of the proletariat" sees to it that goods and services are equally distributed – in theory, anyhow. In reality, elites call the shots in socialist and capitalist systems alike, and the lower classes are shortchanged. Elitism and social stratification are inescapable, it seems. Or are they?

The social contract, which is the basis of constitutional government, is an attempt made by forward-thinking people to eliminate tyranny in all its forms. It's a relatively new concept, actually, not much older than the Magna Carta drawn up by petty nobles in 13th Century England to check the absolute power of their king. The social contract is the basis of all enlightened governance. It leads to a burgeoning middle-class and political stability. The social contract is a civil inclination designed to humanize all our interactions with each other – a collective "We" where every "I" in society is considered important. Yet 10,000 years after the first inklings of civilization, the integration of the "I-You" relationship into social systems still remains a work in progress.

When alone in wild country, I give little thought as to what I should or should not do regarding my fellow human beings. I wander about, wild in the truest sense of the word, looking out for myself and myself only. At such times, I feel as free as any creature can feel. But it doesn't last. Eventually, I must return to the developed lowlands and interact with my own kind again. Those interactions, both social and economic, are fraught with peril. I can't acquire food or basic amenities without doing business with others. A complex set of relations comes into play during the process, involving me with millions of other people around the globe. I can't fill the gas tank of my car without having a hand in wars being fought in distant lands. I can't replace my tattered shirt without the issue of sweatshops arising. My well being in integrally tied to that of every other person on this planet, whether I like it or not. This is where our civil inclinations have led us since the first seeds were planted.

Humankind has globalized. There's no point arguing about whether this is right or wrong. It's simply the way things have evolved over time and, as history shows us time and again, things don't always make sense. As Simone de Beauvoir once said, "It is no more necessary to regard History as a rational totality than to regard the Universe as such." History is a record of actions taken by individuals, small groups, and larger entities such as kingdoms and corporations. In many ways, human history is no different from natural history. Both show only what has happened, not what could or should have been. As human beings, we control our destinies to some extent, but always there remain factors beyond our control. Human nature is still a part of nature, and nature is wild and unpredictable.

In deep woods reverie, I often pine for the days when the number of people on this planet was counted in millions instead of billions. Those were the good old days, I tell myself, when there was plenty of room for everyone. I would have enjoyed living towards the end of the last Ice Age, I think. After all, I would much rather face down a saber-toothed tiger with nothing more than a spear in hand than fill out the tax papers that land on my desk every year. I would much rather go hungry for a day or two than jump through all the hoops necessary get a passport or driver's license. But that doesn't mean my distant ancestors had it easy. On the contrary, their lives were brutal and short. Had I been around fifteen thousand years ago, I probably wouldn't have lived past the age of forty. And there's no sense comparing the quality of life back then to what I enjoy today.

So civilization, it seems, is a double-edged sword – good for some things and not so good for others. I must admit that I've seen a net benefit from it. But is this true for everyone? Certainly not. Perhaps, in due time, the social contract will maximize the benefits of civilization while minimizing its pitfalls, and globalization will see to it that no one is left out. Whether things turn out this way or not, there's no going back to that simpler time when there were just a few widely separated bands of us with stone tools, facing down wild animals, and contending with the elements. For better or worse, those days are gone forever. Our civil inclinations have seen to that.

Humanizing the World

For most of human history, the name of the game has been survival. Widely scattered bands of *Homo sapiens* struggled for existence during the Ice Age and the years that followed, just like every other life form. There were times, no doubt, when the fate of our kind seemed in question. Not any more. Now we are nearly seven billion strong and still multiplying. We have beaten the elements, outsmarted all other animals, domesticated the better part of the earth, and checked many of the deadliest microbes. On average we live longer, healthier lives than our distant ancestors. In short, we are one of nature's great success stories.

We are everywhere now – deep in the equatorial rainforests, at the poles, and all points between. We inhabit the deserts, mountains and steppes, as well as the fertile river valleys where we first got ahead in the game. We move easily through all of nature's realms now: land, sea and air. We are even starting to leave the planet. Who knows how far we can take it? Perhaps someday, we'll inhabit other planets. What's to stop us?

A hundred years ago, nearly everyone assumed that the resources on this planet were unlimited, and that extracting them was just a matter of time and ingenuity. Oh sure, there were those who talked doom and gloom even then, but few people took them seriously. As far back as the 18th Century, an Englishman named Thomas Malthus had forecasted an ecological apocalypse. In his book, *Population: the First Essay*, he had warned that, "The power of population is indefinitely greater than the power in the earth to produce subsistence for man." His main argument was an exercise in simple math. Population, when left unchecked by external forces, increases exponentially while foodstuffs can only increase arithmetically. In other words, multiplication trumps addition – a truism, certainly. But a hundred years ago, when there were only a billion and a half people on such a large and bountiful planet, this warning was ignored. The Malthusian doom-and-gloom scenario and those who preached it were dismissed as pessimists.

Several decades ago, just about the time our population broke the five billion mark, some scientists claimed that the desertification of the planet and human activity were closely related. But don't worry, we were told by others, technology will save the day. Technology would solve the problem of growing population and shrinking farmland before the situation became too serious. The Green Revolution, as it was called – better seeds, fertilizers, and pesticides – would fix everything. And so it has to some extent. Yet Malthusian math still threatens.

A little over a decade ago, just about the time we broke the six billion mark, the vast majority of the world's scientists agreed that the current warming of the planet was most likely due to human activity. There are people around today who still scoff at this notion, but it's becoming increasingly more difficult to deny the causal relationship between the emission of greenhouse gases by power plants, factories, homes and autos, and the overabundance of these gases in the atmosphere. With large, populous countries like China and India rapidly industrializing, this potentially dangerous situation can only worsen. In other words, humankind is fast becoming the victim of its own success.

Pollution remains an ongoing concern, drinking water has never been more precious, and the air in our cities can be downright toxic at times. A mass die-off of other species is currently underway as well – the likes of which the world hasn't seen in a very long time. The deserts are expanding, glaciers are melting, and wildfires are becoming more frequent and ferocious. Tropical storms are more powerful than they used to be and weather is changing on a planetary scale, thanks to oceanic phenomena like "El Ninõ" that we don't completely understand yet. What's going on? Why can't we stop these changes? Why is Mother Nature being so difficult?

In the mid-20th Century, Joseph Wood Krutch wrote: "If in one sense man is now more like a god than he ever was before, he has in another sense become less godlike than he ever previously imagined himself to be." We are *Homo sapiens* – Man Who Knows. We now know enough about the world we inhabit to know just how much more there is to learn. Most of us experience this firsthand whenever we read about the latest scientific breakthrough. On a personal level, I knew everything when I was 18 years old, but with each passing year I seem to know less and less. Once a god, now I'm a mere mortal. So it goes when one pays attention, learning just enough from past mistakes to acquire some semblance of wisdom.

Wise enough to realize how unwise we are – that's where we are today. Our species has arrived at a critical juncture where we know better than to think we know it all. We have reached a point where it's clear that we either check our population and our endless appetite for simplistic solutions, or suffer the consequences. Mother Nature isn't all that impressed by our technological prowess, and she has never been one to go easy on a delinquent species. To maintain a standard of living even remotely close to what

71

we currently enjoy, we must adapt to her in brave new ways. Either that or seriously consider leaving the planet.

The most pertinent question we can ask ourselves these days is this: Is humanizing the world the best course of action?   Obviously we are quite capable of making a profound impact upon this planet, but can we control nature and is that really in our best interests? There is much talk nowadays about stewardship. The preservation of remaining wild plants and animals seems to depend upon it. But I can't help but wonder if the wild can survive our management. Perhaps something will be lost in the process. More to the point, if we micro-manage all of nature, can anything wild still exist here?

"A tamed wilderness will subject itself to man," Loren Eiseley once said, "Not so the wilderness beyond the stars or concealed in the infinitesimal world beneath the atom." I concur.   There's more to wild nature than sanitized documentaries about the animal kingdom ever show. There's more to nature than what we see on The Weather Channel: volcanoes, wildfires, earthquakes, great storms and the like.   In the incredible hubris that he demonstrates, Know-It-All Man tends to ignore that which doesn't fit into his nice, tidy worldview. This is especially true regarding that part of nature refusing to bend to our will. Some call this a defeatist, pessimistic interpretation of things – one that grossly underestimates human ingenuity – but I think reality bears it out.   Yes, we can move mountains, but we can't make them disappear. Oh sure, we can split atoms, but who knows how to clean up the resulting mess? And yes, we can see countless planets out there beyond our own solar system, but how do we reach them without that journey becoming a one-way trip?

There comes a point in the evolution of every species when consolidation is more important than expansion, when survival means finding a niche and filling it. This is demonstrated in wild nature time and again – in the very small, the very large, and everything between. But this fact seems to be lost on us. For some reason, we find it difficult to imagine ourselves having a place *within* nature. It is either us or them, where "them" is everything in existence that's not yet under our thumb. Either we completely humanize the world, turning all wild forests into tree farms, all grasslands into gardens, and making all the earth's creatures our pets, or we fight nature to the bitter end. With us there is no compromise, no middle ground, no simply taking our place in the web of complex relations. No, we're too good for that.

Humankind is a tremendous success story, at least as far as population increase and planetary conquest goes. But can we truly prevail? Can we overcome our own self-destructive tendencies? Keep in mind that we are the last of a long line of brainy bipeds, that the entire genus *Homo* has been reduced to a single surviving species. It could be that Mother Nature's experiment with *intelligent* life forms hasn't really worked out. All this gray matter might be more trouble than it's worth. Perhaps it's time to try something else. She doesn't seem to be too invested in any particular version of existence. While we're busy congratulating ourselves about all the progress we've made since the Ice Age, Mother Nature might be moving in an entirely new direction.

There is much talk nowadays about how we are destroying this planet. There are even those who think it's inevitable that we will render Earth an empty shell and be forced to migrate elsewhere. But I believe that being earthbound is an essential part of who/what we are, and that without this world we would lose our identity. I suspect that if we ruin this planet, wiping out all wildness here, some vital aspect of ourselves will perish as well. Then *Homo sapiens* will join that long list of plants and animals that have come and gone.

Some other version of *Homo* will persist, no doubt. It matters little to nature whether that surviving creature is truly human or something else. The wild will persist in the universe, regardless what happens to this planet or humanity. Mother Nature doesn't care about the particulars, about what comes or goes. The whole is all that matters to her. So it's up to us, really, to determine whether we will survive another 100,000 years, or perish in a mess of our own making during the next few hundred.

There is something deep within me, something very Darwinian, that doesn't want to shrug off the future of my kind. It's the wild in me, no doubt, asserting itself into the world, wanting to persist no matter what. Perhaps there are still enough people like me left on this planet to turn things around. Perhaps we will prevail here even while much more optimistic people are leaving for other planets. Time will tell.

Nature and Existence

We still look to the clear night sky and marvel at the universe as our ancestors did fifteen thousand years ago. In some ways, we are wiser than they were, having a better understanding about what it is that we are seeing. We know that shining before us are countless stars like our own Sun, countless galaxies like our own Milky Way, and a great sprawl of space reaching back to the beginning of time. But in other ways, we are just as mystified as they were by the incredible forces at work in the universe. We still stand with mouths agape before the unknown, longing for a level of understanding that can never be, more aware now than ever before that every major breakthrough in knowledge only generates more questions. As *thinking* creatures, we are resolved to know as much as we possibly can, to push back the unknown as far as it will go, even while accepting the harsh fact that our grasp of things will always come up short. This, it seems, is our destiny.

The strictly rational thinkers among us would like to discard the idea of God. Others are not so quick to believe that we live in an utterly logical universe, where the laws of nature are both immutable and mathematically comprehensible. Some of us see dynamic forces at work in nature – a tension between order and chaos – and fall to our knees in deep reverence for it. Oddly enough, those who call themselves believers in God harbor the same desire for complete order as rationalists. It is the existence of chaos in nature, it seems, that disturbs them most – religious and secular thinkers alike. God or mathematics? It matters little to most people what kind of laws give nature its structure as long as those laws remain sacrosanct. But in the quantum world nothing is absolute. In Darwin's nature, the wild in all its bizarre manifestations defies all simplistic interpretations. According to Darwin and those who fully grasp the implications of his theories, nature is dynamic.

"It is God's nature to be without a nature," the Christian mystic Meister Eckhart once wrote. I think the same can be said about nature itself, if one cares to differentiate between the two. This is where the wild comes into play. The wild is precisely that aspect of God and/or nature that we cannot anticipate, let alone organize. It is altogether human to desire perfect understanding, to search for an overriding scheme to the universe, but what we desire and what we get are two different things. With each passing century, we grow a little smarter as a species, but the unknown is always with us. Therefore every philosopher remains somewhat in the dark, and something of a shaman.

For the more scientifically inclined, there will always be some riddle of the cosmos begging further investigation. In his book, *Pensées*, the French philosopher, mathematician, and scientist Blaise Pascal wrote: "Nature is an infinite sphere whose center is everywhere and circumference nowhere." Well put. This statement is as true as any statement about the universe can possibly be. Once again, pure logic is confounded by the irrationality of the infinite. Careful now. Talk of infinity quickly degenerates to God-talk. If you want your formulas to remain tidy, keep away from the infinite by all means. It confounds mathematics every time.

Nature *is* existence. This statement, an obvious tautology, suggests that whatever we find in the world must in some way be a part of it. Yet human beings, nature's highly skilled craftsmen, are constantly manipulating the raw materials of the world into completely new things. We commonly use the terms "manmade" and "artificial" to distinguish what we have created from what is natural. This is one of those places where we get into trouble, where logic breaks down. All things exist in nature, yet something can't be both artificial and natural at the same time. Can't have it both ways. Or can we? Herein lies the fundamental paradox of being human, of being both a part of nature and separate from it.

As much as anything arising from our blank canvases, pottery wheels, or foundries, our humanity is largely of our own making. Curiously enough, the wildness within us – that which binds us to nature – is the wellspring of all creative energy. We mimic God, creating the world anew each day, breathing our will into lumps of clay and altering existence accordingly. We are human therefore imaginative, innovative. There is no limit to what we can do, make or think. Our abstractions make us immortal. And yet, like all animals, we are born, eat, reproduce, and die. Strange, isn't it? That among nature's many mysteries, being human is the greatest mystery of them all.

The world doesn't make sense. Neither do we. That human beings walk the earth defies all logic. That a creature capable of uttering the word "infinity" could emerge from the long march of evolution, well, it's an accident beyond all probability. What reason could there possibly be for such a creature to exist? Mother Nature, it seems, is always ready to throw a curve ball, always ready to try something new, to do something unexpected. We would be wise to keep this in mind the next time we try to define her. Clearly she doesn't want to be defined.

All our greatest accomplishments are the products of abstract thought, yet now we risk becoming the victims of abstraction. In the Age of Information, it is too easy to lose sight of nature, to miss the forest for the trees. It is too easy to focus on the many social, political and economic problems we have created for ourselves and forget that the world itself is not our invention. That is why we need great big swatches of wild country, where laptops, cell phones, and other techie toys are irrelevant. We need these places not as vacation getaways, but as psychological and spiritual sanctuaries – places where we can go and reconnect with What-Is. Otherwise we are doomed to live in a world utterly of our own making, where all things appear to be under our thumbs. The consequences of losing such wild places would be devastating. As goes the wild, so goes the human.

We would be wise to keep in mind that no matter how much we live inside in our heads, we remain inexorably linked to nature. As Gary Snyder reminds us, "Nature is not a place to visit, it is *home*." How easy it is for us to forget that. How easy to ignore the robins searching our carefully groomed yards for worms as we hop in our cars and go to work. How easy to see a wildflower in a ditch and call it a weed, or miss seeing it altogether. We do not go *out* to nature. We live and breathe it every moment of our lives. To forget this is to lose that sense of perspective critical to our collective long-term survival.

When I was alone in the Alaskan bush, I enjoyed a moment in which I felt perfectly at ease. A small campfire burned smokeless at my feet, the river nearby flowed past incessantly, bald eagles screamed nearby, and I was at peace with the world. All around me a mist gathered in forested mountains. In the distance the sun reflected off glaciers older than civilization. In that moment, I could have been a shaman wrapped in skins and grasping a stone tool instead of a bespectacled philosopher with pen and paper in hand. Then I realized that that Ice Age hominid and I are one in the same, that this magnificent world is where I belong. I live in it, try to make sense of it, marvel at its wonder and beauty. To be human is to be an integral part of nature. No matter what we do or how deep into space we venture, we'll be okay as long as we keep this in mind.

Notes

The Known and the Unknown

"Religion is the attempt..." Rudolph Jordan, *Bridges to the Unknown* (Frederick Fell, 1957) p. 26.

"I too began to contemplate the possibility that the earth moves. To be sure, it seemed an absurd idea." Taken from a letter from Nicholas Copernicus to Pope Paul III, *The Book of the Cosmos*, edited by Dennis Richard Danielson (Perseus Publishing, 2000) p. 107.

"May God forgive Galileo..." Giorgio de Santillana, quoting Pope Urban VIII, *The Crime of Galileo* (Time Inc., 1962) p. 235.

"The most valued facts..." Chet Raymo, *Honey From Stone: A Naturalist's Search for God* (Hungry Mind Press, 1999) p. 151.

"I think therefore I am." René Descartes, from "A Discourse on Method", *The Rationalists* (Doubleday, 1974) p. 63.

"I do not agree with the view..." Stephen Hawking, *Black Holes and Baby Universes and Other Essays* (Bantam, 1994) preface, p. viii.

The Quest for Meaning

"The sage hatches no schemes..." *Chuang Tzu: Basic Writings*, translated by Burton Watson (Columbia U. Press, 1964) p. 71.

"One day the 'why' arises and everything begins..." Albert Camus, *The Myth of Sisyphus* (Alfred A. Knopf, 1955) p. 10.

"Reason and the irrational..." *The Myth of Sisyphus*, p. 35.

"Man's search for meaning is a primary force..." Victor Frankl, *Man's Search for Meaning* (Pocket Books, 1963) p. 154.

Wild, Wilderness, Bewilderment

"The naturalistic principle forbids us to believe that there ever occur interruptions in the natural working of events or capricious interventions by a supernatural being." W. T. Stace, *Mysticism and Philosophy* (Tarcher, 1987) p. 23.

"How can I withstand..." Martin Buber, *Pointing the Way* (Harper, 1957) p. 60.

"I have discovered..." John Muir, *The Wilderness World of John Muir*, edited by Edwin Way Teale (Houghton Mifflin, 1954) p. 311.

The Sharp Edge of What-Is

"You cannot understand..." Indries Shah, recounting a discussion between Sufi mystic Simab and a nobleman named Mulakab, *Thinkers of the East – Teachings of the Dervishes* (Penguin Books, 1972) p. 109.

"Listen to the voice of the wind..." Rainer Maria Rilke, *The Selected Poetry of Rainer Maria Rilke*, translated by Stephen Mitchell (Random House, 1982) p. 153.

"Heaven is under our feet..." Henry David Thoreau, *Walden* (Apollo Edition, 1966) p. 375.

Unmasking the Laws of Nature

"The foregoing generations..." Ralph Waldo Emerson, *Nature* (Beacon Press, 1989) p. 5.

"God does not play dice." Taken from the Einstein/Born letters by Michio Kaku, *Beyond Einstein* (Anchor Books, 1995) p. 47.

"It is difficult to decide where science..." Banesh Hoffman, *The Strange Story of the Quantum*, (Dover, 1959) p. 177.

The Impossible Cosmos

"This year, humanity learned..." Astronomy Picture of the Day (December 31, 2003) http://apod.nasa.gov.

"Philosophically, the notion of a beginning..." Arthur Stanley Eddington, excerpt in *The Book of the Cosmos*, edited by Dennis Richard Danielson (Perseus Publishing, 2000) p. 403.

"The big bang idea..." Fred Hoyle, excerpted from *The Book of the Cosmos*, p. 411.

"If you admit the existence of time..." Moses Maimonides, quote taken from *The Book of the Cosmos*, p.84.

"By the name God..." René Descartes, from "Meditations", *The Rationalists*, p. 137.

"What is it that transforms..." Thomas S. Kuhn, *The Copernican Revolution* (Harvard Univ. Press, 1976) p. 76.

The Emergence of Life

"...the conception of spontaneous generation..." A. I Oparin, *Origin of Life*, (Dover, 1953) p. 3.

"Life is so great a mystery..." John Burroughs, *Accepting the Universe* (Fredonia Books, 2001) p. 260.

"Mystery generates wonder..." Ursula Goodenough, *The Sacred Depths of Nature* (Oxford Univ. Press, 1998) p. 13.

A Web of Complex Relations

"A struggle for existence inevitably follows..." Charles Darwin, *The Origin of Species* (Penguin Books, 1985 reprint) p. 116.

"...are bound together by a web of complex relations." *The Origin of Species*, p. 124-5.

"Introduce design into nature..." John Burroughs, *Accepting the Universe*, p. 48.

"The universe endures..." Henri Bergson, *Creative Evolution* (Dover, 1998) p. 11.

On Being Human

"Who is man? ... he is a being..." Abraham J. Heschel, *Who Is Man?* (Stanford Univ. Press, 1965) p. 28.

"Man is nothing else..." Jean-Paul Sartre, *Existentialism* (Philosophical Library, 1947) p. 18.

"...the keynote of all humanistic problems." Susanne K. Langer, *Philosophy in a New Key* (Harvard Univ. Press, 1957) p. 25.

Civil Inclinations

"Simple cultures normally belong to small societies and complex ones to large." Elman R. Service, *Origins of the State and Civilization* (Norton, 1975) p. 306.

"One basic word is..." Martin Buber, *I and Thou* (Scribners, 1970) p. 53.

"It is no more necessary..." Simone de Beauvoir, *The Ethics of Ambiguity* (Citadel Press, 1972) p. 122.

Humanizing the World

"The power of population..." Thomas Malthus, *Population: The First Essay* (Ann Arbor Paperback, 1971) p. 5.

"If in one sense man..." Joseph Wood Krutch, *The Measure of Man* (Charter Books, 1962) p. 31.

"A tamed wilderness will subject itself..." Loren Eiseley, *The Unexpected Universe* (Harcourt Brace Jovanovich, 1969) p. 42.

Nature and Existence

"It is God's nature..." Meister Eckhart, *Meister Eckhart: A Modern Translation*, translated by Raymond B. Blakney (Harper & Row, 1986 reprint) p. 243.

"Nature is an infinite sphere..." Blaise Pascal, *Pensées* (Penguin Books, 1966) p. 89.

"Nature is not a place to visit..." Gary Snyder, *The Practice of the Wild* (North Point Press, 1990) p. 7.